Finding
GOD
when the
World's
on FIRE

Copyright © 2016 by Charles R. Swindoll

Published by Worthy Inspired, an imprint of Worthy Publishing Group, a division of Worthy Media, Inc., One Franklin Park, 6100 Tower Circle, Suite 210, Franklin, TN 37067.

WORTHY is a registered trademark of Worthy Media, Inc.

HELPING PEOPLE EXPERIENCE THE HEART OF GOD

eBook available wherever digital books are sold.

Library of Congress Cataloging-in-Publication Data

Names: Swindoll, Charles R., author.
Title: Finding God when the world's on fire : strength & faith for dangerous
    times / by Charles R. Swindle.
Other titles: Why, God?
Description: Franklin, TN : Worthy Publishing, 2016. | Includes
    bibliographical references.
Identifiers: LCCN 2016038601 | ISBN 9781617958113 (tradepaper)
Subjects: LCSH: September 11 Terrorist Attacks, 2001. | Terrorism--Religious
    aspects--Christianity.
Classification: LCC BT736.15 .S95 2016 | DDC 242/.4--dc23
LC record available at https://lccn.loc.gov/2016038601

Unless otherwise noted, Scripture quotations are taken from the New American Standard Bible. Copyright © 1960, 1962, 1963, 1968, 1971, 1972, 1973, 1975, 1977, 1995 by The Lockman Foundation. Scripture quotations marked NIV are taken from the Holy Bible, New International Version®, NIV® Copyright ©1973, 1978, 1984, 2011 by Biblica, Inc.® Used by permission. All rights reserved worldwide. Scripture quotations marked NLT are taken from the Holy Bible, New Living Translation, copyright © 1996, 2004, 2015 by Tyndale House Foundation. Used by permission of Tyndale House Publishers Inc., Carol Stream, Illinois 60188. Scripture quotations marked NKJV are taken from the New King James Version®. Copyright © 1982 by Thomas Nelson. Used by permission. Scripture quotations marked KJV are taken from The Holy Bible, King James Version. All rights reserved.

For foreign and subsidiary rights, contact rights@worthypublishing.com

978-1-61795-811-3 (Trade Paper)

Cover Design: Melissa Reagan
Interior Design and Typesetting: Bart Dawson

Printed in the United States of America

17 18 19 20 LBM 8 7 6 5 4 3

Finding
GOD
when the
World's
on FIRE

STRENGTH & FAITH
for **DANGEROUS TIMES**

CHARLES R.
SWINDOLL

WORTHY
Inspired

CONTENTS

ACKNOWLEDGMENTS

WHEN A FIRE BREAKS OUT in a field not far from your home, you feel uneasy. If the wind picks up and starts to blow in your direction, your uneasiness quickly grows into panic. Knowing how helpless you are to fight the flames alone, you need others to step up and help out. Before that fire reaches your house, you start to grab things most important to you, then you make your getaway. If that fire continues to grow, destroying other homes in your neighborhood, all of you will go through the same exit strategy without planning any of it ahead of time. As you drive away at breakneck speed, you cry out to God, pleading with Him to do what you cannot do . . . to rescue you from further danger, to turn the direction of the wind, to stop the inferno before it destroys everything in its path.

Speaking of infernos, on September 11, 2001, our country caught on fire. Brutal terrorists started the blaze as more than three thousand perished. Since then, the winds have picked up speed and are now blowing in our direction. The flames of terrorism at home and abroad are out of control. Our need is not only to find safety; *it's to find God*!

Our entire world is now on fire. We hope to survive, but that's an impossible plan if we operate alone. We need help—help from God as He tells us what to do. Once that happens, we need to handle this inferno exactly as He instructs.

So, I have called on others to help me put out the flames. First, I chose Byron Williamson and his publishing team at Worthy Publishers to help me get this book into print and distributed far and wide. I thank all of them for their splendid assistance in fighting these flames.

Next, I asked my longtime friend, Mark Tobey, to provide his editorial assistance, as he has on previous occasions. In spite of his own demanding schedule and deadlines serving in our Creative Ministries Department at our Insight for Living Ministries, he stepped into this fiery task. Matt Yates, who serves with his father, Sealy, as my literary agent, also did his part with excellence. With mutual determination, we fought the flames together.

Now, here's the result. Working together, we've found God in our flaming world, and we've listened to His advice. I hope you will too. May you soon discover that you have no reason to panic. God has everything under control—even this.

ONE

FINDING GOD WHEN THE WORLD'S ON FIRE

And you must show mercy to those
whose faith is wavering.
Rescue others by snatching them from the flames.

Jude 1:22–23 NLT

There's something about
the human heart,
that when the heat is on,
it softens toward things
of the Lord.

DEVASTATING FOREST FIRES don't suddenly erupt full force—they ignite with a spark and expand.

All of us can recall in our minds the bleak images of a raging fire consuming thousands of acres of forests and homes as high winds and extremely dry conditions combine with all things flammable to create a fiery monster, upending the lives and threatening the livelihoods of countless unsuspecting people.

As enormously devastating as these conflagrations become, forest fires, like all fires, begin and progress in a short series of eerily predictable stages.

First, there is the *incipient* stage—where the fire initially ignites. Extremely dry conditions and elevated temperatures combine with some outside element, usually very small. A half-smoked cigarette flipped into a patch of dry weeds. The inevitable burst of sparks from an evening campfire landing randomly on dry underbrush, half a mile away. A bolt of lightning from a summer storm hitting the arid ground. The fire begins *incipiently*.

Next comes the *growth* stage. Soon the smoldering ember whips into a flame that then begins its insidious advance across the dry, wooded area, vacuuming up oxygen and heat and dry particles from its surroundings—*growing* into a moving and ever-increasing wall of fire.

The third stage follows as the fire becomes *fully developed.* In this stage, the fire is at its hottest, most dangerous level—spreading rapidly, at times up to twenty or more miles per hour—consuming everything combustible in its path. Firefighters fear this stage most because of what they refer to as the dreaded "flashover" phenomenon, when a treacherous wall of fire can literally leap a barrier, as if in a daring surprise attack, and overwhelm those furiously battling the frightening advance.

Finally, fires enter what's called the stage of *decay.* This is the point at which the flames begin to die out, either because of moister, cooler conditions, or because the fire simply runs out of consumable fuel sources. Still, the danger lurks, because this is the stage when a "backdraft" can occur, as oxygen drifts back into still volatile, confined spaces and reignites the flame.

WHEN THE WORLD'S ON FIRE

Evangelist Billy Graham was prophetic in his instincts when he wrote, decades ago, his powerful volume, *World Aflame.* In it, Dr. Graham warned of a coming time in history when life as we know it would be consumed by evil. That evil wave—like a forest fire—would begin incipiently, virtually unnoticed, but eventually, unchecked, it would blaze across our culture with devastating results.

Most of us who were quietly going about our festive Thanksgiving celebrations in November of 2015 still remember the shocking images broadcast on our television screens—bloodied corpses strewn across a large concert hall in downtown Paris. Several hooded and heavily armed radical Islamic terrorists had stormed into the loud and darkened music venue and had gunned down patrons in cold blood, shouting allegiance and praise to Allah.

Remember that dreadful scene? The longer that night dragged on, the more clearly the horror of what had actually unfolded came into view. The footage being broadcast from Paris was absolutely gruesome. . . . We couldn't believe our eyes. When I heard that ISIS had quickly taken credit for the hideous ordeal, a tingling chill shot up my spine. *If they can make it to Paris, what stops them from coming here? If we're not even safe going to a musical concert, then why would we think it's okay to go to a mall?*

The raging flames of Islamic terrorism have grown into a fully developed forest fire of fear, mind-boggling violence, and a seemingly complete and total disregard for boundaries to its destruction.

In shock, we ask, *Are You there, God?*

I have lived to see presidential assassinations, prejudicial assassinations, political assassinations, and horrible suicide attacks. I watch young veterans of our conflicts in Iraq and Afghanistan stumble back to America's shores, many struggling in the grip of post-traumatic stress, unable to rebuild their lives since they are crippled, blinded, or paralyzed from devastating wounds of both the body and the spirit.

I've stared at pictures of Hiroshima and Nagasaki in the wake of the bombing, of deadly explosions in the harbor at Texas City, at the Twin Towers in New

York, at the Boston marathon, and at the US embassy in Benghazi.

With tears welling in my eyes I ask, "O Lord, are You there?"

In my over eighty years on this earth, I thought I had just about seen it all . . . until the brutal beheadings began. Stunningly broadcast live on the Internet—Christians and Muslims, children and fathers, sons and community leaders—mercilessly executed before our very eyes by ISIS, in the name of their diabolic religion of rage.

What started incipiently decades ago as a spark of conflict in the arid deserts of the Middle East has now exploded into a fully

> In shock, we ask, *Are You there, God?*

developed raging fire of sickening evil unlike any the world has ever known, and it is spreading across the continents.

What we believe about the proponents of this violence is that they are evil and demonic. Their tactics are designed to instill terror and paralyzing fear through their repeated and increasingly savage acts of aggression.

The most recent acts of heinous violence demonstrate to the world the limitless depths to which ISIS and other radical Islamic extremists are willing to go to throw even more fuel on the fire.

Yet a question lingers in my mind: *In the midst of the flames, is it possible for someone to find God?* There's something about the human heart, that when the heat is on, it softens toward things of the Lord.

Solomon wrote, "Sorrow is better than laughter, for sadness has a refining influence on us" (Ecclesiastes 7:3 NLT). And "Enjoy prosperity while you can, but when hard times strike, realize that both come from God. Remember that nothing is certain in this life" (Ecclesiastes 7:14 NLT).

The late Ray Stedman, my longtime friend and ministry mentor, once told of a conversation he had with a retired sea captain. The seasoned mariner recounted stories of navigating his ship through wild waters as storms of enormous strength battered his vessel. He told of one particularly intense storm where he wasn't certain anyone on board would actually survive.

"Yes," he sighed, "the Lord heard the voices of many strangers that night!"

I'm convinced God is hearing the voices of many strangers during these treacherous days. Maybe one of those voices is yours. Perhaps in the midst of the raging flames of fear and the searing heat of such perilous times, you are beginning to ask, "Can I find God when the world's on fire?"

I want to assure you, you're not alone.

TWO

WHEN THE FOUNDATIONS SHAKE

The flame shall not hurt thee; I only design
Thy dross to consume and thy gold to refine.

How Firm a Foundation,

Rippon's *a Selection of Hymns*, 1787

Where is God
when the world's on fire?

On Sunday night, October 8, 1871, the well-known evangelist, D. L. Moody, preached to the largest congregation that he had ever addressed in Chicago. His text that evening was, "What shall I do then with Jesus which is called Christ?" (Matthew 27:22 KJV). At the conclusion of his sermon he said, "I wish you would take this text home with you and turn it over in your minds during the week, and next Sabbath we will come to Calvary and the Cross, and we will decide what to do with Jesus of Nazareth."

Moody's song leader, Ira D. Sankey, stood to lead in singing the hymn,

> *To-day the Savior calls;*
> *For refuge fly;*
> *The storm of justice falls,*
> *And death is nigh.*

Sankey never finished the hymn. While he was singing, the rush and roar of fire brigades sounded from the streets outside the church, interrupting the service. Before morning, much of the city of Chicago lay in ashes.

What had incipiently begun as a small fire in a farmer's barn rapidly grew into a raging conflagration that overtook the city in a matter of hours. Many lost their lives; countless others, their entire possessions.

The great D. L. Moody never fully recovered from the regret of not calling people to repentance that very night. In his own words, Moody confessed:

"I have never since dared," he said, "to give an audience a week to think of their salvation. If they were lost they might rise up in judgment against me. I have never seen that congregation since. I will never meet those people until I meet them in another world. But what I learned that night which I have never forgotten is when I preach, I will press Christ upon the people then and there and try to bring them to a decision on the spot. I would rather have that right hand cut off than to give an audience a week now to decide what to do with Jesus."[1]

As a preacher, I can relate to Moody's burden. The burden of offering people truth when life swings in the balance. Almost without exception, rarely has a month gone by in recent times when we've not witnessed the smoldering aftermath of another brutal terrorist attack, another car bombing, another dreadful downing of an airliner filled with hundreds of unsuspecting travelers, another murder of a police officer, another rampage on students in their school, or another village brought to its knees by the barbaric advance of ISIS. Preachers like myself are forced to wrestle with the tension of continuing in what we've been teaching or turning our attention once again to the question at hand: *Where is God when the world's on fire?*

Images remain indelibly cauterized in my mind of the hours and days following the September 11, 2001, terrorist attack on multiple targets in the United States—the Twin Towers being the most notable. The remnants of the towers, an entire section of the US Pentagon, and an obscure grassy field in rural Pennsylvania lay smoldering in ashes for days. It was yet another "day of infamy," times three.

On the weekend following that horrific day, every

preacher I know—in fact, most preachers across the globe—scrambled to change their sermons for Sunday, September 16, 2001.

The series that I was presenting at the time on the life of the apostle Paul suddenly seemed irrelevant in light of our back-to-back tragedies. Like all the other pastors, I changed direction and immediately began to peruse the events in which we found ourselves, in hopes of finding some calming words for our chaotic times.

It is amazing how history repeats itself.

And just like the Sunday following the events of September 11, 2001, I find myself again lifting those words of hope from the ancient yet ever-relevant book of Psalms.

THREE

FEAR OR FAITH?

I trust in the LORD for protection.
So why do you say to me,
"Fly like a bird to the mountains for safety!"

Psalm 11:1 NLT

If our foundations
are in place, then
nothing else really matters.

Cynthia and I lived in Southern California for almost twenty-five years. I recall how often I was amazed at the frequent forest fires that ravaged the land. Fortunately, we did not experience any loss from these fires, but we knew some who did. Since moving to Texas, I still feel a familiar pang when the newscasts report that the California fires have ignited again, or similarly, as I listened recently to reports of the massive Fort McMurray fire in Canada. What is equally tragic are the many who ignore the warnings to evacuate.

In 2003, more than twenty people lost their lives in a series of fires where the flames moved faster than many residents could flee. When people complained that officials didn't offer enough prior warning, Sergeant Conrad Grayson responded, "We're begging people to leave, and they don't take us seriously. . . . The ones who listened to me left the area and lived. The ones who didn't, died."[2]

The only prudent response to a dire warning is to flee. That's certainly true when you find yourself in the path of a raging, out-of-control forest fire. But what about when circumstances in your life make you feel out of control?

Psalm 11 is the place to go. It was written by David, Israel's shepherd king, at a time when his life began to feel unhinged. He was being hunted and haunted by King Saul, who was determined to kill him. David's words offer insight into the reality of fear and the contrasting power of faith.

David had received a word of warning from a close advisor, urging him to run for the hills like a bird flying to the mountains for safety. Instead, David paused and considered a compelling question: "If the foundations are destroyed, what can the righteous do?" (11:3 NKJV).

Great question! Webster tells us that a foundation is "the basis upon which something stands or is supported." Every house has a foundation. Every significant structure, every multiple-storied high-rise has a foundation. The taller the building, the deeper and more substantial its foundation. Destroy the building's foundation, and you've toppled everything.

A particularly devastating strategy of ISIS has been to move into the areas they overtake and begin destroying the foundations of that particular culture. Historical monuments and long-standing remains of ancient structures as well as intricately preserved works of art and architecture are systematically leveled by the terror group. Not only has the landscape been irreversibly altered, the collective psyche of the inhabitants of these lands has been forever ravaged and diminished.

Foundations are everything. If our foundations are in place, then nothing else really matters.

That is precisely David's point in Psalm 11. David is not referring to literal structures or great works of art or even layered stones that comprise enormous fortress walls. David's psalm is about standing firm in life when one's entire world seems on fire, when devastation seems imminent.

The righteous—people whose lives are rightly related to God by faith in Jesus Christ—stand on a firm foundation.

Now, should the foundation of a life be destroyed, that life crumbles. But if the foundation remains secure, no amount of stress—in David's case, no brutal attack on his life by Saul or painful backstabbing from his own son Absalom—would cause his life to fracture or ultimately crumble. David envisioned those threats as arrows coming from warriors. In his psalm, he uses a vivid word picture: "The wicked are stringing their bows and fitting their arrows on the bowstrings. They shoot from the shadows at those whose hearts are right" (11:2 NLT).

In those days, the warrior was an excellent marksman, known for his keen ability with the bow and arrow. One of the most effective weapons in David's day was a sharp, slender arrow as it slipped from the bow, guided by the archer's eye to the target. David's point was that the wicked had him secretly in their sights; they were stealthily getting ready to attack.

What a fitting metaphor for our times! We face a constant threat of unseen, spontaneous attacks— terrorists bursting into crowded theaters; suicide bombers standing in long lines of innocent men, women, and children. And then the threat becomes real as the terrorists release their "flaming arrows" of devastating explosives and scattered shrapnel.

We can relate to David's advisors, whoever they

were at the time, by responding in fear and panic a⸱

we retreat. Yet David would have none of

strengthened his resolve to respond in faith, n⸱

He declared at the outset of his psalm, "I ⸱

the Lord for protection," and again, "But the L⸱

in his holy Temple; the Lord still rules from he⸱

He watches everyone closely, examining every pe⸱

on earth" (11:1, 4 NLT).

What a magnificent declaration of confidence i⸱

the Lord his God!

David's soul was definitely not on the run. His

spirit refused to melt amid the encroaching flames of

opposition and danger. His refuge was in the Lord. A

refuge is a place of hiding—a place of secure protection.

The term is *chasah* in the ancient Hebrew. A chasah is

a protective enclosure that provides safety from that

which would otherwise consume everything in its path.

It's an impenetrable firewall of protection from danger

and distress—from anxiety and fear. David makes it

clear that the Lord alone is his chasah. He remained

firm in his confidence in the Lord. His "foundation" of

trust would not be shaken. He was fully human, but he

found incredible stability in his divine refuge.

The old country preacher was right when he said, "I may tremble on the rock, but the rock don't tremble under me." Keep in mind: David has no corner on such confidence. Faith is *our* solid foundation too. A foundation of faith, not fear, is our refuge; it enables us to stand firm against the advancing threats of terror.

> God is our refuge [chasah] and strength, always ready to help in times of trouble.

David's word *refuge* reminds me of yet another psalm—Psalm 46—that includes a remarkable promise we can claim. Who wouldn't find comfort in the solidarity of this ancient promise? This is the very psalm in which Martin Luther, the great Protestant reformer, found refuge and relief more than five hundred years ago. He hid in its truths and found strength when the fires of persecution raged about him. Psalm 46 fueled his courage to go on, even though he was misunderstood, maligned, and mistreated. How comforting are these opening words in Psalm 46:1 NLT: "God is our refuge [chasah] and strength, always ready to help in times of trouble."

It was from the opening lines of this psalm that

Luther was later inspired to write, *"Ein' Feste Burg Ist Unser Gott."* "A high tower is the Lord our God." We who are Christians sing the familiar lyrics today: "A mighty fortress is our God, a bulwark never failing."

Why is such a foundation impervious to the flaming advance of terror and danger? Because our "mighty fortress" is God Himself! Our bedrock foundation is the God of creation who has revealed Himself in the person of His Son, Jesus Christ. The God who made us and saves us is the God who shelters us from danger and calms our fears in threatening times. He's there. He offers us safety. Our need is simply to rest in Him.

He who dwells in the secret place of the Most High shall abide under the shadow of the Almighty [El Shaddai]. I will say of the LORD, "He is my refuge [my chasah] and my fortress; my God, in Him will I trust" (Psalm 91:1–2 NKJV).

On that solid foundation of faith, we are secure. We find help and hope in God—even when the world seems on fire.

FOUR

A VERY PRESENT HELP IN TIGHT PLACES

God is our refuge and strength,
an ever-present help in trouble.

Psalm 46:1 NIV

He is a very present help
in those tight places
of fear and uncertainty.

G od is our refuge and strength. As Eugene Peterson paraphrases it in *The Message*, "God is a safe place to hide." Literally, the Hebrew of this psalm could be rendered, "God is our refuge and strength, a very present help in *tight places*." I like that.

As we said in the previous chapter, the Hebrew word *chasah* is a word we all need as we feel the flames of terror licking ever closer.

The news of ISIS furthering its horrifying reach deeper into the Middle East and more recently into Europe makes even the most stalwart of souls pause with uncertainty.

When I find myself struggling to sleep soundly at night (which has become a more frequent challenge), I bring to my mind the words of Psalm 46, and I remember that wonderful word *chasah*; God is my very present help in tight places. Charles Spurgeon writes,

As God all-sufficient, our defense and our might are equal to all emergencies. . . . He is

not as the swallows that leave us in the winter;
He is a Friend in need, and a Friend indeed.
When it is very dark within us, let brave spirits
say, "Come, let us sing the forty-sixth!"

> A fortress firm and steadfast rock,
> Is God in time of danger,
> A shield and sword in every shock,
> From foe well-known or stranger.[3]

A deeper dive into Psalm 46 brings to us much needed perspective in these perilous times. Like Psalm 11, the forty-sixth begins with a declaration of confidence in the Lord, upon whom the remaining body of the biblical text hangs. In other words, think of the first verse as the coat hanger; all the remaining garments (2–11) hang on that support. The hanger is that God is our refuge and very present help in tight places. When we are uneasy about the future, when anxiety about our times threatens our ability to carry on with normalcy, God is our refuge. When it feels as if the entire world is on fire with threats of terror from enemies and we cannot see or anticipate relief, again, God is our refuge. We need to form the habit of repeating those four powerful words to ourselves: *God is our refuge.*

If you study the structure of Psalm 46, you'll observe the same word used three times. Let your eyes scan through the remaining words of the psalm and notice the right margin. At the end of verse three, selah. At the end of verse seven, selah. And again, at the end of the final verse in the psalm, selah. What's that about?

Selah. Selah. Selah.

The Psalms were originally songs composed to be set to music and to be sung as part of Jewish corporate worship. They provided the lyrics for inspired worship, praise songs, and hymns. Many years ago, the Christian church sang the Psalms—they literally sang words from the Psalms. Think of it this way: David, Moses, Korah, and others provided the first hymnal for the people of God.

I have a very old songbook, if you can call it that. It is comprised of just words from various psalms that were sung centuries ago. In Old English it is titled *The Psalter.*

When God's people gathered, they sang from *The Psalter.* This notation is written at the beginning of

Psalm 46: "For the choir director. A Psalm of the sons of Korah, set to Alamoth. A song." The word *Alamoth* comes from the Hebrew word *almah*, which is translated "maiden" or "young woman." It probably means it was composed to be sung in a soprano voice. So if you can hit the high notes, this psalm was written especially for you!

> He is fully in control, *absolutely* sovereign, not *almost* sovereign.

Keep in mind, it is a psalm of God's chasah. He is our refuge—and what comfort that brings in the midst of the fire! You can find God when the world's on fire. He's not running for cover, nor is He wringing His hands in confusion. Furthermore, He is not worried. God is in the heavens, securely and sovereignly offering a safe place for you to escape and find security, safety, and comfort in your furnace-like trial. That's where you find God—on His throne, thoroughly overseeing each detail of our lives. Isn't that a magnificent thought? He is fully in control, *absolutely* sovereign, not *almost* sovereign.

He is there when troubles surround you. He is your refuge when your son or daughter boards that aircraft carrier bound for the Arabian Peninsula. He is your refuge when terrifying events unfold that you cannot explain or even understand. Should a reign of terror hit our nation, He will be there. He is our refuge and strength. He is there when our children and grandchildren shake in fear because they're beginning to understand what terrorists do and how near they could possibly be. He is their refuge and strength too, to calm their innocent, tender hearts.

All of that and more is included when we say that He is a very present help in those tight places of fear and uncertainty. Selah. We're back to that strange word, selah.

Meaning what? Selah was most likely an ancient musical notation. Music scores today have unique notations. They are like punctuation signs that musicians understand. They signify changes in tempo and volume and even the style the composer originally envisioned. Some appear as small arrows pointing to the right or to the left, others are phrase lines connecting notes and measures to indicate one continual flow of motion.

In biblical days, the word *selah* probably indicated

a pause. A breather, a moment to reflect. I have a friend who, every time he reads the Psalms and comes across this word, provides his own translation: "Pause and let that sink in." I often do that, too . . . and I deliberately pause and stay silent a few seconds.

> In place of worry and anxiety, pause. . . The Lord is our refuge.

The three selahs in Psalm 46 are the structural markers of the psalm. Verses 2 and 3 refer to times of physical catastrophe. Selah. "Pause, and let that sink in. Here's how to handle such things." Verses 4 through 7 refer to the threat of warfare. Selah. "Pause and let that sink in. This is how to respond to that." And in verses 8 through 11, when the future seems uncertain, this is how you handle that. Selah. "Pause and let that sink in."

Don't run ahead; pause.

Don't panic; pause.

Don't fret and fear; pause.

In place of worry and anxiety, pause. The foundation stands firm. The Lord is our refuge. He is our very present help in tight places. Even when the flames seem more like a blast furnace.

Pause and let thoughts of God's absolute sovereignty sink in.

Then keep reading.

FIVE

WE NEED NOT FEAR

*We will not fear, though the earth
should change and though the mountains
slip into the heart of the sea.*

Psalm 46:2

Our God is in sovereign control
of all the events of this earth.

Few of us can even begin to imagine the physical catastrophes that have befallen the thousands of victims of ISIS's ongoing violence and relentless assaults. Horrifying images and even more horrifying reports of the most brutal of executions—including beheadings, crucifixions, burning alive of prisoners, and the sexual and emotional torture of innocent women and children—stream into our living rooms on a frequent basis.

Add to that the eerily increasing occurrences of major earthquakes and raging, out-of-control forest fires, rains and flooding of epic proportion, volcanic eruptions, and ferocious tropical storms that have ushered in untold physical ruin to so many lives across the world. In times like this, what is our response? Usually, it's *Why, God? Why me? Why them? Why us?*

In contrast, God's Word offers this counsel in times of physical catastrophe: "we will not fear." Notice again that the examples given at the beginning of this psalm are all introduced with "though." "Though the earth should change and though the mountains slip into the heart of the sea" (Psalm 46:2). Referring to what? Though there be an earthquake and the ground moves beneath you. "Though its waters . . . foam" (46:3). That would have reference to floodwaters rising and ruining or washing away all your physical possessions and stealing your identity and livelihood. The psalmist goes even further in verse 3, listing another physical catastrophe: "Though the mountains quake at its swelling pride." An avalanche or volcanic eruption! That terrible moment of looking up and watching thousands of tons of rocks and debris or massive amounts of snow and ice plunging toward you. Our response? Since God is our refuge, we will not fear. Is that amazing, or what? We will not fear!

Why not? Let me repeat the promise that secures our foundation. We do not fear because the Lord our God is our chasah—our refuge, our hiding place. He is our strength. He Himself is the rock. All such catastrophes surprise and shock us, but nothing surprises or shocks Him. Our God is in sovereign control of all the events of this earth. They occur exactly as He has planned or permitted them.

Then how can I explain why such terrible things are allowed to happen to innocent people? Why would God allow ISIS and other evil, violent perpetrators to make such significant advances across the Middle East and around the world and disrupt our sense of security and safety? The psalmist does not suggest that God somehow feels compelled to explain Himself in these matters. In fact, I remain convinced that our Father has planned or permitted the events of this earth, inexplicable though they may be. He has no obligation to explain Himself or to justify His reasons. The Creator does not explain why to those He created. It would be like a brilliant potter being obligated to explain himself to a mass of soft clay.

Nothing surprises God. However, He does permit events that often puzzle us, and His reasons are too profound for us to grasp. They are put together in the counsel of His own will, and they fit perfectly into His plan for His glory and for His purposes. As His servant, I say in response, "I will not fear. Though I don't understand it, I will not fear. Though You, Lord, take something that's deeply significant to me, though You allow catastrophe to strike, I will not fear. I will not blame you, I will not doubt Your goodness, and I will not question Your intentions."

That means there will be no out-of-control anxieties. Why? Because God is our refuge. There will be no exaggerated feelings of uneasiness. Why? Because God is our refuge. There will be no middle-of-the-night shakes. Why? Because God is our refuge. There will be no dread or lingering depression. Why? *Because God is our refuge.*

Martin Luther connected those dots:

And though this world with devils filled,
Should threaten to undo us,
We will not fear, for God hath willed
His truth to triumph through us!

The answer is not complicated. Selah. Pause, and let that sink in. Rest easy. Don't expect life always to make perfect sense. Don't fear because surprises occur. Life is full of surprises, shocks, and insanities.

One night some time ago, I was feeling disturbed over the current atrocities being perpetrated by ISIS and the pending dread that one day such horrors could reach my state or my city and threaten the security and safety of my family. The more I wrestled with those thoughts, the more anxious I became over the probability of domestic terrorist attacks on innocent, defenseless people in my own community. For quite some time, I tossed and turned in bed, unable to drift back to sleep.

I will not doubt
Your goodness, and
I will not question
Your intentions.

I got up, walked upstairs into my study, slumped into my rawhide leather chair, and stared at my shelves of books. The small lamp we leave lit through the night gave me enough light to read one title after another.

Suddenly, my eyes shifted to my computer screen. I noticed an unopened e-mail message from a long-time friend who lives in Southern California. I clicked into it and was relieved. Among other things, he asked a simple question: "Have you noticed the insights in Psalm 94:19?" Curious, I opened my Bible and read the verse: "When my anxious thoughts multiply within me, your consolations delight my soul."

I blinked and read those words again. Talk about

a selah moment! I had to pause and let that statement sink in. A surge of refreshing peace came over me. My anxious thoughts were eclipsed by a peaceful confidence that God was in control and understood exactly my need. The final result? My soul was delighted. His Word again reminded me that He alone is my refuge and strength. I went down nineteen steps, went back to bed, and slept soundly until dawn.

But there is more, much more, in Psalm 46. What about warfare? All Jews looked upon Jerusalem in those days as the "city of God" (46:4). So David, as he's hiding in the rocks not far from the great walled city where he's spent so many years of his life, pauses and reflects. He remembers the river that flows into the channels that irrigate the soil. He pictures in his mind's eye the crops and plants that grow in the wilderness region, thanks to the quietly flowing water. He calls the city the "holy dwelling places of the Most High" (46:4). In David's psalm, God again emerges as paramount—*God* is the star of the event. "God is in the midst of her," he exclaims. Regardless of what forces threaten the city of God, "She will not be moved" (46:5).

We are not moved either. We are not moved, even

though terrorists have come at us with their atrocious attacks; though they continue to launch their tactics of fear against the civilized world; though they bring anxious thoughts to the minds of our children and grandchildren. We are not moved because "the LORD of hosts is with us; the God of Jacob is our stronghold. Selah" (46:7). Remember: pause and let that sink in.

In the midst of all these violent, terrifying ordeals, our tendency is to scroll the Internet news streams more often than we read the Bible. Am I right? Haven't you spent much more time watching cable news broadcasts in recent days than you have spent reading God's Word? We tend to be more familiar with the faces and names of newscasters on Fox News and CNN than the encouraging words of David in the Psalms. Because that is often true, we easily forget, "The LORD of hosts is with us; the God of Jacob is our stronghold" (46:7).

- How can I be sure?
- How can my family not be anxious?
- How can I combat fear?
- How do I face such a dangerous, uncertain future head on?

Verse 8 of Psalm 46 invites us: "Come." It says, in effect, "Come here, *pssst*. Come back here for a moment." God offers us an invitation in times of uncertainty to travel back into history. To return to a former time, a bygone era. To blow the layer of dust off our memory.

Come, behold the works of the LORD, who has wrought desolations in the earth. [Remember the past.] He makes wars to cease to the end of the earth; He breaks the bow and cuts the spear in two; He burns the chariots with fire (Psalm 46:8–9).

Those accounts of God's former deliverance flow from the chronicles of biblical history. Mentally scan the grand narratives of Genesis, Exodus, Numbers, and Joshua. As you do that, observe the frequent examples of God's strong and faithful arm, moving on behalf of His people. Against the backdrop of such a witness of God's faithfulness, you can read one strident report after another of a town or region overwhelmed by ISIS or witness the atrocities of yet another people group terrorized by the maniacal whims of a self-aggrandized warrior and claim this promise with confidence: "We will not be moved."

God declares, "I will be exalted among the nations, I will be exalted in the earth" (46:10). David concludes this section by repeating the statement he used earlier: "The LORD of hosts is with us; the God of Jacob is our stronghold. Selah" (46:11).

We will not fear, though catastrophes continue to occur. We will not fear, though we are at war with an ideology we simply cannot fathom. Why? Because God—the omnipotent, all-knowing, and magnificent God—is our refuge and strength. And He is with us.

Get it? Got it? Good!

SIX

CONFIDENCE IN UNCERTAINTY

Cease striving and know that I am God.

Psalm 46:10

God's Word became
the ammunition to weaken
the enemy's position
and strengthen the Christian's.

For years I've been fascinated by tales of the great nineteenth-century North American explorers Meriwether Lewis and William Clark. These courageous and calculating ambassadors set out across an unknown wilderness in search of a passage from the uncharted interior of America to the sparkling shores of the Pacific Northwest. It was a harrowing journey that included remarkable stories of survival from the threat of wild animals, Indian ambushes, raging rivers, bone-chilling blizzards, and yes, forest fires. One journal entry from the expedition captures a particularly spine-tingling episode. (By the way, these men were magnificent explorers but terrible spellers!)

The Prarie was Set on fire (or cought by accident) by a young man of the Mandins, the fire went with such velocity that it burnt to death a man & woman, who Could not get to any place of Safty, one man a woman & Child much burnt and Several narrowly escaped the flame. A boy half white was saved unhurt in the midst of the flaim. . . . The course of his being Saved was a Green buffalow Skin was thrown over him by his mother who perhaps had more fore Sight for the protection of her Son, and less for herself than those who escaped the flame, the Fire did not burn under the Skin leaving the grass round the boy. This fire passed our camp last [night] about 8 O-Clock P.M. it went with great rapidity and looked Tremendious.

—October 29, 1804, *William Clark Journal Entry*[4]

That's the nature of a forest fire—it starts incipiently, then accelerates rapidly into a raging inferno of mind-boggling intensity. Most people who have encountered and narrowly survived these flaming monsters testify to the paralyzing aspect of fear. Countless times, people have lost their lives, not out of stubbornness toward the clear and present danger but because of fear. When fear seized them, it paralyzed them so completely that they were unable to face reality with a deliberate and calm resolve.

Like fear of a raging fire, anxiety about the future

can paralyze our faith and render us immobilized, unable to face an uncertain future.

So how do we deal with the intense anxiety that grips us when we're anticipating an uncertain future? What enables us to press on with inner confidence in spite of the violence of ISIS, the cataclysmic episodes of nature's fury and destruction, and the weakening of the once-solid foundation of religious and political freedom?

Verse 10 of Psalm 46 announces the answer. *We will not worry.* The psalmist writes, "Cease striving." The Hebrew uses a single term in that command that means, literally, "stop!" What a great directive. ***Stop!***

You can almost imagine the Lord of heaven thundering this command to His people as they shrink in fear: "*Stop. Stop it. Stop worrying about the future! Have you forgotten that I am your very present help in tight places? Your worry and fear imply that I am no longer here or that I have become impotent and out of touch. But I am not indifferent. Nothing has escaped My panoramic gaze and powerful control. I'm not like the swallows that flutter away in the winter, to return only when the weather clears.*"

Now you can see why Psalm 46 speaks with such relevance. In times of physical catastrophe, because God is our refuge, we will not *fear*. At the constant threat of war, because God is our refuge, we will not be *moved*. Even with a future that is so uncertain, we will not worry. We'll remember He brings an end to war. War is nothing new to our God. The implements of war are frightening to us—chariots, spears, arrows, car bombs, hidden explosives, handheld weapons. All have a way of intimidating us and making us churn within. God commands, "*Stop!*" We will not worry.

I love stories about the Revolutionary War, when our nation first fought for independence. In those days when immense strife spread across our land, it wasn't uncommon for pastors to preach sermons that prepared their congregations for battle; I mean literal battle. There was a war going on, and sermons were delivered to instill courage in the hearts of those who would leave the pews and soon be on horseback, engaged in the fight for freedom. Those sermons came to be known as "artillery sermons." What a great name! When a pastor preached with passion, you could almost hear the report of the artillery: *Kavoom! Kavoom!* The pastor's launching another artillery sermon today—*Kavoom!* I love that!

Artillery sermons were preached by stouthearted, unintimidated pastors, who also served as leaders of the local militia. Back then, artillery was the first-strike weapon; it led the infantry attack. Heavy cannons were designed to weaken the enemy's defense for the assault. In a similar way, artillery sermons were delivered to stir hearts and prepare people for battle. God's Word became the ammunition to weaken the enemy's position and strengthen the Christian for literal as well as spiritual warfare.

If it would help you to think of this book in that way, consider this to be one of those *kavoom* messages. This is an artillery message, because some who may be reading this book have been nearly paralyzed by fear. You've been fearing for your safety when you travel; you're worried about the world your children and grandchildren will face when you're gone; you're anxious about an imminent terror attack in your

> Because God is our refuge, we will not *fear.*

neighborhood. But fear can overtake you only when you haven't been equipped with the proper ammunition. In fact, no terrorist is able to destroy or defend against the truth of God found in His Word.

If the foundations are in place, if the Lord our God is your refuge and strength, then you can *cease striving and know that He is God.* He is not moved. He is not distant or disinterested. Those who trust in Him stop worrying, as fear is sent packing.

KAVOOM!

SEVEN

IDENTIFY
THE ENEMY

Your enemy the devil prowls around
like a roaring lion looking
for someone to devour.

1 Peter 5:8 NIV

We can resist the enemy—
even battle him—
and be victorious.

Fighting a raging forest fire takes careful planning followed by decisive action. Reconnaissance is key.

Before any major action is taken to battle the blaze, critical information about the type of fire is essential. Is it a crown, ground, or surface fire? You need to know specifics related to the geography and topography of the fire's path, wind direction, and escape routes for the firefighters. Information regarding critical air support and any other unexpected contingencies is gathered in order to mount the most effective approach to conquering this insidious enemy. Knowing the nature and potential next moves of the blaze safeguards against surprise backdrafts, devastating losses, and injuries.

The same is true in battling the ever-present and stealthily unpredictable enemy of radical Islamic terrorism. ISIS represents a more ruthless, sophisticated, and financially supported organized terror group than any other we've witnessed. They have no limits in the form or extent of human suffering they will cause or terror they will perpetrate in order to accomplish their diabolic intentions.

Yes, you read that correctly. *Diabolic.* I'm convinced ISIS and all other like-minded terror organizations are ultimately ruled and directed by the unseen "ruler of the kingdom of the air" (Ephesians 2:2 NIV). I'm referring to none other than Satan himself.

He not only directs the terror on the worldwide scene, he is the originator and chief architect of the evil forces that relentlessly attack our minds and assail our hearts every day of our lives. Yes, you also read *that* correctly.

"Your adversary," the apostle Peter reminds us, "is the devil." He is at the root of all evil. He stops at nothing to engage in an ongoing strategy to bring us down. With deceptive stealth, he's "like a roaring lion, seeking someone to devour" (1 Peter 5:8). But before you can launch any counterassault on this ruthless enemy of your soul, you have to know who he is. It's called reconnaissance—you must be able to identify him in all circumstances. Once again, the Word of God is our guide.

When I did a serious and thorough investigation of

the Scriptures on the nature of the devil, I discovered he was the highest of all angelic creatures. Though he fell from that exalted position due to pride, he didn't lose any of his brilliance. Make no mistake about it, when the highest of God's angelic creatures fell, he dropped like a flaming spark to the dry, sin-prone undergrowth of the human experience and lit a fire that has expanded into a raging inferno of evil. Small wonder that we're told to "be of sober spirit" (5:8). The battle to fight his incipient ways is on! Once we identify the enemy and understand his wicked ways, we realize the entire world is threatened by his fiery advances.

Let me pause here and set the record straight. First, we're living in a culture that is politically correct but theologically uninformed, ethically compromised, and morally corrupt. To the very core of its being, today's culture is corrupt. Humanity without Christ is totally depraved. The earth's evil system (called the *kosmos* in Greek) conspires to keep you from finding God when the world is on fire. It will lead you directly away from God instead of point you to Him for refuge. If I were David the psalmist, I would add to that statement: Selah. Pause and let that sink in!

Second, we are facing hardships, conflicts, terror, and worldwide disruptions like none of us would have ever imagined, because we are encountering our adversary on his turf. Everything God's people love, he hates. For instance, he hates your lifelong commitment to your marriage. Chances are good that more marriages are in conflict in these fearful days than in times past. Chances are you've got more troubles than usual in your family, troubles rooted in anxiety and its kissing cousin, fear. Perhaps one or more of your children is in open rebellion, trapped in addiction, or struggling with issues related to their gender identity, spurred on by an insane free-for-all culture that promotes unlimited freedom and sexual deviance. Or maybe you are buried in a mountain of debt, having bought the lie that more is always better and you "deserve" every happiness, regardless of whether you can afford the cost.

Why the struggle? Our adversary hates a peaceful, harmonious family. He relishes strife and division.

Chances are the conflicts occurring in your occupation have reached such an intense level, you're ready to say, "I don't know if this faith stuff really works anymore. Where is God in all this mess?" The confusion, doubt, and chaos are all part of the enemy's insidious strategy.

We should expect enemy attacks in any number of areas. While we ought not to live in fear of them, we're not to be ignorant of them either. The enemy loves for you to be kept ignorant and oblivious to the advancing danger of his flaming attack. He hates messages like this book that warn and equip you. They identify him for who he really is; he doesn't go for that.

> The shield of faith will protect you . . . like a firewall.

Ready for some good news? It's found in this same section of Scripture. We can resist the enemy—even battle him—and be victorious! Look closely and read carefully the opening line of 1 Peter 5:9: "But resist him, firm in your faith." The enemy's attacks may be directed toward the vulnerable part of your life, but the shield of faith will protect you from them like a firewall. Trust the scriptural promise. You *can* resist him.

Furthermore, realizing that God is your refuge, you can call on Him immediately. You can find God when the world's on fire by turning to Him in prayer and humbly asking Him for help. There's absolutely nothing like finding God's very present and personal help through prayer to dislodge the enemy's fiery darts. Good news: You're not alone in your struggle. Verse 9 declares "your brethren" (other people just like you) are experiencing the same sufferings as you are. You're not unique. Others near you and on the other side of the world are feeling the same mix of fear, anxiety, doubt, and confusion and are wondering to themselves, *Where can I find God in all this?*

God is there, and He can be found. Yet the enemy desires that you remain isolated, feeling anxious and without hope, so that you'll easily fall under his horrifying spell. He'll do everything in his power to keep you from finding God, to leave you feeling stranded and alone.

My task is to equip you, point you to truth, and prepare you for what is ahead in the struggle. You can be sure, the reasons for concern will not diminish any time soon. In fact, such troublesome things will only intensify as the battle continues to rage.

When you find your hope and refuge in God, you will not worry. You will not succumb to the power of fear. Best of all, you will not fall unknowingly into the enemy's hands.

In the amazing book of Revelation at the very end of the Bible, the apostle John, the author, vividly describes the enemy, his attacks, and the ultimate outcome. The war has already been won by the good guys. When Jesus died on the cross and rose again, it was all over for Satan, the enemy. His fiery rage was forever extinguished by the downpour of mercy and grace in Christ's death and resurrection! He was and remains ultimately defeated and doomed. He knows this, but still, he fights on. His embers of fear and terror still smolder, awaiting a fresh whip of oxygen to reignite his fury. Ultimately, however, it doesn't matter, because he's lost the war. He knows that too!

John reveals a fiery end to the enemy of our souls when he writes these triumphant words: "And the devil who deceived them was thrown into the lake of fire and brimstone, where the beast and false prophet are also; and they will be tormented day and night forever and ever" (Revelation 20:10). That's your adversary's final destination.

Until then, the battle against him continues, and

we must resist him and continue to fight. Like the myriad brave men and women in uniform spread across the globe, standing against the relentless advance of terror, we too must march into battle against the forces of fear and anxiety, armed with the courage that only comes from the written Word of God. As we go, we know we are already victorious!

Are you ready to fight?

EIGHT

CLEAR DIRECTION FOR TREACHEROUS TIMES

Humble yourselves, therefore,
under God's mighty hand,
that he may lift you up in due time.

1 Peter 5:6 NIV

The Lord's direction for us
in these perilous times is
"humble yourselves."

It wasn't there when a few men gathered around him. On that early June day in 1944, General Dwight Eisenhower had the unenviable task of deciding if that was the right day to make the most significant invasion in the history of military strategy.

The weather wasn't right.

The tide wasn't right.

The sea wasn't good.

The counsel wasn't anywhere near unanimous.

The general had hoped for agreement. It wasn't there. In fact, some of his most trusted advisors urged, "No." But he said, "Let's go."

As we all know from history, he made the right decision. However, those first few waves of soldiers were picked off by the enemy like sitting ducks. The wet sand on that beach was dyed crimson with the blood of those brave Americans as they invaded the northern perimeter of France before moving on toward Berlin.

I have the distinct feeling that nobody sat around in a small group telling jokes just before those first few waves hit the beach. No one in an amphibious landing craft said, "Man, is this fun, or what? We're gonna have the time of our lives." No, not that morning. Those were real bullets in their rifles. Those were real shells in every massive Nazi cannon. To make matters worse, there were powerful landmines hidden along those now infamous shores.

Bodies were blown apart. Friends died horrible deaths. It was serious stuff as they waded ashore. Some stumbled to find cover; others were blinded by deafening explosives, scared half out of their wits. They knew this was for keeps. No more jokes, no more fun and games. Those few weeks of training were done. This was the real thing—raw, brutal, life-and-death combat.

Isaac Watts's words may be old, but they have a twenty-first-century ring of relevance. Consider the questions he asks in his timeless hymn entitled "Am I a Soldier of the Cross?"

> *Are there no foes for me to face?*
> *Must I not stem the flood?*
> *Is this vile world a friend to grace,*
> *To help me on to God?*

Do you see the questions? Do we have foes? Can we escape the flames in this world on fire? He answers firmly:

Sure I must fight if I would reign;
Increase my courage, Lord;
I'll bear the toil, endure the pain,
Supported by Thy word.

In this time when our entire world feels as if it's a bonfire, smoldering here and there from the fiery advance of radical Islam and paralyzing economic tremors, we face very real threats. In ISIS and other like-minded terrorist groups, we have very real enemies. To make matters worse, the source of all that heinous evil is invisible, as are many of the entities and their forces that threaten to undo us. Some still question Satan's existence—even as his rage continues to assail the earth. Rarely are "artillery sermons" delivered in the pulpits of our land anymore. How seldom are Satan and his demons even mentioned by name? In many churches today, you hear virtually all of that explained away: "*This isn't like that!*"

We are led to believe that this "ancient foe" is a mere figment of our imagination, a creature with a red epidermis and horns, carrying a pitchfork and sitting like an imp on our shoulders, whispering evil thoughts and suggestions. No! This enemy is not only real, he's brilliant. *Genius* is a better word. He's been studying you for all your years. He knows you thoroughly and plans an attack that will strike at your most vulnerable weakness in hopes of bringing you down. He exists for your failure, fall, and ultimate destruction.

In order to cut through the smoke of his fiery advances, we need clear direction in these flammable times.

The words of the apostle Peter come to mind. In 1 Peter 5, we find battle terms that sound like marching orders—clear and unmistakable direction for all of us who desire to follow our Commander in Chief, Christ. But the initial command is surprising. Rather than "Attack!" it's "Humble yourselves" (5:6). We need to understand—this isn't human strategy based on human strength that requires human giftedness to lead to human accomplishments. This is altogether contrary to what any of us would imagine. The Lord's direction for us in these perilous times is "Humble yourselves." Peter paints a picture of falling on your face before God in submission and trust. Trace "humble yourself" back as far as possible, and you will find people literally on their faces before God. The word picture includes God's almighty, outstretched hand reaching across this universe—including this tiny planet and including His church—which He brought into existence by His power and for His purposes.

God commands us to humble ourselves under His hand. This means you and I don't get our own way. It isn't about getting what we want. When you humble yourself under the Master's hand, you humble yourself to the Master. It's about doing what He wishes. It's what He plans that matters. You hardly need to be told that everything in our culture works against that simple, clear direction. No matter. The command stands: "Humble yourselves under the mighty hand of God, that He may exalt you at the proper time" (1 Peter 5:6).

There are rewards for doing as He commands. God is no divine sadist; He doesn't watch people squirm and struggle and bleed, hoping to club them into submission. The evils we experience, the threats we face that are very real these days, are not divine retribution for our past sinful deeds. Don't go there. Keep in mind that God—our loving and caring, holy and just God—has shaped a plan that will lead to victory, hope, peace, and joy. All of it takes shape under His mighty hand as we surrender our wills to His. It happens *under* His hand. Get that. Under His hand, we give up what we want. We surrender our wishes and our desires, and we accept His plan. In the process, He is glorified. Because of His grace, many rewards come our way. The blessings just keep coming, like waves on the seashore. They come at "the proper time," because His timing is always right.

> Keep in mind that God has shaped a plan that will lead to victory, hope, peace, and joy.

You say, "That kind of full surrender to someone else's plan makes me nervous." I understand; believe me. But that's why Peter included another exhortation in verse 7: cast "all your anxiety on Him."

"You mean, I might not get what I want?"

No, you will often not get what you want. Life will not always go your way. If that makes you anxious, there's a simple solution: Cast all your anxiety on Him, yes, all of it. When you do, you will have a lot less struggle in releasing your will to Him. You'll face the advancing flames of confusion and difficulty with far greater confidence and much less fear.

What I'm suggesting here is a completely different lifestyle than what our culture promotes. This will touch every part of your world. In the final analysis, it will lead to a 100 percent investment in Him.

Perhaps I'm hearing you say, "Well, I don't want to invest, say, my whole life."

Let me cut to the chase: If you resist that, you really don't want Christ. You aren't looking to find God in these anxious times. Because the only way to find God and experience His peace is to bring your entire mind and will into full submission to Christ, His Son. You're really looking to find a God who doesn't make such wholesale demands. That way, you can hear what you want to hear and do what you please. You want a God who makes you laugh, makes you feel good, and grants your every request.

You say, "Man, this is getting serious." Yes, you're right.

Peter tells us to be sober, to be on the alert. We're to follow God's clear direction and obey His orders. The first one is clear: humble yourself. If you do, when the time comes to face the battle, He will lift you up with sufficient confidence and courage to conquer the enemy.

Days after radical Islamic terrorists attacked the World Trade Center in New York and the Pentagon in Washington, DC, on September 11, 2001, I sat alone in my study, contemplating what had struck our nation. I was saddened by the horror of it all and later gladdened to see our country fall to her knees before God and humbly ask for His protection. I was grateful for the humility it brought to all of us. But I was troubled that it had taken such an evil, savage event to bring us down to where we needed to be . . . not just then, but all the time.

How quickly we have forgotten and reverted to our self-sufficient ways in the years since 9/11. Today as the flames of terrorism have been reignited in ISIS and other radical groups, we once again feel the heat from threats that are beyond what any one of us can imagine. It is time to obey our Commander's orders. It is time once again to humble ourselves under His mighty hand. To accept His strategic plan, to submit and surrender to Him.

Once we do, we will find in Him the courage to move out in His name. The soldier who advances on his or her knees never retreats.

NINE

A COURAGE
TRANSFUSION

Be on the alert, stand firm in the faith,
act like men, be strong.

1 Corinthians 16:13

Be alert!
Stand alone!
Grow up!
Get tough!

The challenge we face is painfully acute. Our foundations are in place and reliable. The Lord our God, being our refuge and very present help, relieves us of fear and worry. He is in complete control. He hasn't lost His grip on our times, though it might feel at times as if He has. Under His mighty hand, we humble ourselves. In spite of our adversary's subtle and deceitful strategy, we are certain of this: *In the end, God wins.* It's difficult now, but ultimately, God will gain the victory. What we need in the meantime is a courage transfusion.

I want to offer you eight words from the statement of the apostle Paul in 1 Corinthians 16. I hope you never forget them. I will present these words in an unusual way. I'll present four two-word commands that will be simple to recall. These commands are found in verse 13 of 1 Corinthians 16: "Be on the alert, stand firm in the faith, act like men, be strong." Each one of these two-word commands deserves a bold exclamation point.

Here's the first command: *Be alert!* When Paul first wrote this command, he put it this way: "Keep on watching!" Clearly, those passionate commands urge us to be acutely aware. That awareness includes spiritual awareness, an awareness of the unseen, an understanding of our adversary's insidious presence, and a quick perception of satanic conspiracy. The enemy is at work among us, so stay alert!

As we learned in previous chapters, there is an ongoing diabolical conspiracy against the plans and purposes of God. It has been going on since before the fall of humanity in the garden of Eden. Satan and all who operate under his authority hate God's plan and God's people. The first thing the enemy would love for you to believe is that there really is no such thing as a conspiracy. Yet it exists, without question. Be on the alert when you read the newspaper, scroll through an Internet article on current events, or listen to a live cable news broadcast. Listen and reflect on these things with a keen, biblical discernment.

These treacherous times require a keen discernment that must kick in, in full force. Parents, guard your children from an overexposure to news broadcasts of a disturbing and terrifying nature. Younger children are extremely susceptible to fear that can develop as a result of their eyes and ears being bombarded by such things. Teach them to know what's wholesome and what isn't.

Christians, be alert to what is going on around your community, in the schools of your area, among politicians—local, state and federal . . . in fact, all the way to the Oval Office. Pay particular attention to matters related to national elections. Prayerfully consider the options before you respond. Be alert to extremes and follow the Spirit's direction.

God says, "*Stay alert!*" Stay alert to biblical principles. You will often discover them when you open God's Word. You will hear them on Sundays if you attend a Bible-teaching church. Such biblical principles will guide your steps, relieve your fears, and temper your responses. Pay close attention to them. Remember them. Apply them. Mentally repeat them to yourself. *Be alert!* That's the Lord's first counsel of defense for us. Be keenly and discerningly aware.

Second, *Stand alone!* It is rendered here in 1 Corinthians 16:13 as "stand firm in the faith." Eugene Peterson says it this way in *The Message*: "Hold tight to your convictions." You may have spent years listening to preaching. You may have taught the Bible in small groups in your home or at your church. Perhaps you are engaged in training new believers. If so, stand firm in the truth you have been teaching. When necessary, stand alone.

Don't let it bother you that you are different or that you're in the minority. Don't worry that your convictions brand you as politically incorrect or socially intolerant. Don't let that cause you to shrink from what you believe. Stand tall. Step up. Stay strong.

I can assure you of this: The mentors who shaped me and my ministry were stronghearted individuals who stood firm in what they believed. They never walked back from anything they taught, and they never bored me (or anyone else) with their biblical teaching. Some were quirky, some were outspoken, and some were opinionated. But all of them stood firm.

Don't concern yourself with how others run their companies or rear their children. Run yours right; rear your children as God has led you according to His Word. Don't care if most of the people walk away from danger, shrink back in fear, or sell out to culture. You

walk toward it. Face it with courage and solid con-
viction. You do what is right. Don't lie. Don't cheat.
Don't steal. Don't hang around with people who do. It
takes courage to swim upstream against the current of
complacency. Swim upstream, anyway!

Third command, *Grow up!* If the first two commands haven't been strong enough, this third one
should grab your attention. "Grow up!" These are two
words you probably haven't heard lately. Paul says it like
this: "Act like men." I know you're an adult. But age
proves little in tough times. Maturity is what's needed
in the hour of decision. This command compels us
to be wise and rational adults in things that matter,
like taking responsibility, thinking clearly, and acting
courageously in these perilous times.

You may be a parent with children in a public
school. You're facing the weirdness of the political cor-
rectness agenda. You may have kids whose friends are
struggling with identity/gender issues. Don't go off the
deep end. Remain calm in your response. Be firm in
what you believe, but be calm and gracious with your
words and wise in your approach. That's what maturity
in Christ looks like. Mature men and women refuse to

allow their emotions to hijack their reactions. Be salt and light, not poison and gun powder!

By the way, the words "act like men" appear only here in all the New Testament. That makes this a unique command for all of us. It's as if the Lord is pushing His finger against our sternums and asking, "Isn't it about time you took full responsibility for your actions and reactions? Doesn't it seem right for you to align your life with My Word?" Yes, it's time.

> Allow the Lord to transform those long-held negative attitudes that do nothing to advance His cause.

When you commit a wrong, admit that. If you're the one who caused the issue, own it. That's what adults do. If you promise someone you'll do something, then do it!

By the way, it's childish to resist change. Growing up is the goal for those who are in Christ. Do you need to change? Since you're an adult, grow up and change! Allow the Lord to transform those long-held negative attitudes that do nothing to advance His cause. They only hold you back from accomplishing His purposes in your life.

It's really time to do these things! Especially now that so much is at stake in our world. It includes standing down from everything being about you. Growing up means making certain your life is calibrated toward serving others.

One of the greatest men who ever led a seminary was the late Dr. John F. Walvoord. He served as president of Dallas Theological Seminary for thirty-four years. At his ninetieth birthday, I recall a group of us singing "Happy Birthday to You" with pipe organ and trumpet accompaniment. The entire canticle ended with a resounding Presbyterian "Amen" at the closing of our celebrative festivities. It was wonderful. He stood there with a big smile, gazing out at everyone. Looking at him, I realized what a model of maturity he had been throughout his adult life.

When I told that story to a friend not long ago, he reminded me that the great missionary statesman, George Mueller, at age seventy-two, left the orphanage he had founded and placed the leadership in the hands of his son-in-law. Mueller then went on to travel the world, including seven tours of Europe, during which he spoke openly of Christ to the czar of Russia and to the emperors of China and Japan. He also brought spiritual encouragement to the queen of Denmark. He then went to be with the Lord at age ninety-five, while preparing to preach God's Word that evening. I call that modeling maturity all the way to the end!

We need more people like that today—individuals (whole families, even) willing to spend their lives and invest their resources for the glory of Christ, not only in their own tight radius of familiarity but across the street, across the states, and across the seas. The times in which we live are tough, so they require tough-minded maturity.

Stay alert! Stand alone! Grow up!

The last command won't surprise you at all: *Get tough!*

I didn't write "Get mean." I wrote "Get tough." Look at how Paul expressed it: "Be strong."

Have you ever played for a team led by a coach who wasn't tough? If so, do you remember what you did all season? You lost! Great coaches are tough-minded, really strong of heart. As a result, they attract great talent and bring out the best in their gifted athletes.

If you're a preacher or otherwise engaged in communicating biblical truth, you proclaim what *needs* to be proclaimed, not what others *want* you to proclaim. You stand tough even if they don't want to hear it and even if they run you off. Being tough, you stand like a steer in a blizzard.

We're living in a world that's on fire, remember. It's so twisted you can begin to think perversion is actually a virtue. In a culture like ours, being strong will prompt some to call you a bigot or a hateful person, though neither is true. In fact, the accusation is ludicrous! But that's our "world on fire"—into which we are called to *be strong!* It won't be easy, but it will be rewarded.

> The times in which we live are tough, so they require tough-minded maturity.

I was digging around a dusty old bookstore several years ago, and I came across a little volume on the life of the great composer Ludwig van Beethoven. He was some kind of man. Amazingly, the man composed some of his greatest works after he lost his hearing. Eventually he went stone deaf. Once his hearing was completely gone, he had to rely more and more on the feeling in his fingers. At times he would even rest his forehead on the piano to feel the vibrations of what was being played. At one time, in a frustrated moment, he slammed both fists on the keyboard and shouted, "I will take life by the throat!"

I call that great advice for our times! We must take life by the throat. That's *being strong* in the face of such perilous times. Stay alert! Stand alone! Grow up! Get tough!

That's what we must do, both as loyal followers of Christ and as good citizens of our country. Now is the time for a courage transfusion. We must remain alert against the enemy. We must stand alone against the evil, even if others choose not to do so. We must grow up as people with convictions—stand tall, act like mature men and women. And we must be strong— not mean, not paying back evil for evil—but strong in character and stout in convictions. Meet the challenge. Face the flames with faith, not fear.

Yet there remains one final, often overlooked, but enormously potent weapon in our battle to face the encroaching evil. It may not even be something you've wrestled with before now. But it is essential for all of us to embrace and employ as we head courageously into the fray.

TEN

THE FINAL COMMAND

Let all that you do be done in love.

1 Corinthians 16:14

It is love that compels us
into the flame.

You've identified the enemy, received clear, unmistakable direction, and been energized by a fresh infusion of courage. Now what? Surprise assault? Storm the battlefield with guns blazing? Raise your picket signs and your shrill voices in loud protest? "The fight is on—we're ready!"

There's a final command in 1 Corinthians 16:14, and it's none of the above. "Let all that you do be done in love."

LOVE! Always love! *Whiplash!*

That's not expected. That's not what we want to do. He's kidding, right?

We are compelled to love everyone—even our enemies. Yes, our enemies.

Love is the ultimate offense.

Let me tell you who needs your love the most—those who are out of touch with God. Those who are lost. Those closest to you—around the corner, on the street, in the workplace, the parents of your kids' closest friends. Truth be told, we often have difficulty loving even our fellow Christians. Then we attempt to haul our crippled principles and toxic attitudes to the lost world and lecture them on their excesses and lifestyles . . . and all that falls flat and fails, every time.

Why doesn't it work? Because they are lost; they don't have Christ. They do not need our pious principles shouted in their faces. They certainly don't need our sneering condemnations or ugly retaliations. They need the Savior's redeeming love to touch them deeply and to hold them close and to draw them to Himself, to change them from within.

Do you recall how *you* came to know Christ? Again, let's return to words from the apostle Paul: "Do you show contempt for the riches of his kindness, forbearance and patience, not realizing that God's kindness is intended to lead you to repentance?" (Romans 2:4 NIV).

If it was God's wonderful kindness that brought us to repentance, then that same kindness ought to be our ultimate strategy. Every time. Allow true love, God's kindness, to find its way through all of these commands we've been considering. It is remarkable how potent a weapon love is against the enemy's fierce and relentless tactics. (Read that again.)

We are together in this fight. We're like links in a long, strong chain. But we are only as strong as *your* link in that chain. We're only as alert as *you* are on your watch. We stand only as tall as *you* stand when you're alone. We are only as mature and wise as *you* are as a grownup Christian. We are only as tough as *you* are when you face resistance. We're only as loving and kind as *you* are when you interact with and encounter those who are neither.

That kind of love cuts through the fog of prejudice and fear when it comes to reaching out to those who have fallen prey to the adversary's confusing schemes. My longtime friend and ministry mentor, the late Dr. Howard G. Hendricks, often told his students at Dallas Seminary, "Lost people are *not* the enemy. They are *victims* of the enemy." That is so important for all of us to remember as we face down the irrational attitudes and actions surrounding the violence of ISIS; as we debate caring for and sheltering Syrian refugees and other displaced innocent families; as we invite those with broken lives into our spacious homes, including homeless teens or single mothers hit hard by life's assaults. It's good for us to remember when our teenagers, in the name of Christ, befriend a classmate struggling with identity issues or battling a painful addiction. Such demonstrations of love are never forgotten.

Love compels us to run counter to our natural instincts to "flee as a bird to our mountain" and, instead, be led by the Spirit. Remember the wholesome fruit that comes from Him? Love (there's our word), joy, peace, patience, kindness (there it is again), goodness, faithfulness, gentleness, and self-control. You'll find these in Galatians 5:22–23. And here's the kicker: *against such things there is no defense*! We render the enemy virtually powerless when we move toward lost people with these qualities—which, by the way, cannot be mustered from the flesh. Such responses won't come naturally to you, certainly not as you watch the nightly news broadcast! You will be tempted to react naturally out of fear and anger and prejudice. Resist that. Respond in love; be filled with the fruit of the Spirit.

> Lost people are *not* the enemy. They are *victims* of the enemy.

That's how we push back the encroaching wall of Satan's raging fire. One person, one family at a time, as they encounter in us and in our families the irresistible kindness of Christ. His love initially shocks them, then ultimately, it transforms them.

Our country and the free world surrounding us stand shocked, offended, and amazed at the brutality of ISIS and other radical Islamic groups, and rightly so. We are angry. We watch as innocent people are gunned down in cold blood—loving Syrian and Iraqi Christians, men, women, and children—tortured and beheaded for all the world to witness. It's both horrifying and terrifying.

Yet, in the final analysis, it is the love of Christ that infuses us with courage and wisdom to endure the spreading flame and face down the enemy. At the same time, Christ's love moves quietly and powerfully through us into the lives of the lost people we encounter every day in our neighborhoods, in the schools our children attend, on the campuses of our colleges and universities—and it brings about transformation.

It is the love of Christ delivered through us into our terrorized world that dries our eyes, stiffens our backs, and strengthens our resolve to represent Him in our personal lives, as well as in our ministries. It's Christ's all-conquering love that wins the ultimate battle—not anger or hate or retaliation.

It's the love of Christ that keeps us faithful and strong, even while we wonder, *Where is God when the world's on fire?*

I close with words of an obscure New Testament writer—quietly stationed like a sentinel, standing guard at the end of the Bible. His name is Jude. He wrote only one brief New Testament letter—a single chapter that encapsulates our mission. Read his words thoughtfully, preferably aloud.

> *But you, dear friends, by building yourselves up in your most holy faith and praying in the Holy Spirit, keep yourselves in God's love as you wait for the mercy of our Lord Jesus Christ to bring you to eternal life.*
>
> *Be merciful to those who doubt; save others by snatching them from the fire; to others show mercy, mixed with fear—hating even the clothing stained by corrupted flesh.*
>
> *To him who is able to keep you from stumbling and to present you before his glorious presence*

without fault and with great joy—to the only God our Savior be glory, majesty, power and authority, through Jesus Christ our Lord, before all ages, now and forevermore! Amen. (Jude 1:20–25 NIV)

It is love that compels us *into* the flame. Don't you see it? Can't you feel it? It's the power of love. Christ's love compels us all.

LET IT ALL SINK IN

*May God be gracious to us and bless us
and make his face shine upon us. Selah.*

Psalm 67:1 NIV

Let us pause
in the calm for prayer.

Our Father, we are bowed before You, our Great God who offers peace when so many panic. You are our refuge, our *chasah*. Rivet that into our minds, dear Father. Show us how to pause and let Your truth sink in. Remind us of Your power and presence when songs in the evening change into the fearful tears of the night. Remind us of that when the sudden phone call awakens us. Remind us of that when we scan the morning headlines or listen to an unsettling news broadcast about another frightening wave of terror. Remind us, even when we don't understand the why of what's happening, that You can be found among the flames of this world on fire. That You are here and in complete control—seated on Your powerful throne on high—*fully* sovereign, not *almost* sovereign. Remind us that, because of this, we have no reason to fear, that we need not be moved, and that our future is never uncertain with You. May Your love flow through us. We ask this in the strong name of Christ, our Master and Protector and Friend. Amen.

NOTES

1   *D. L. Moody's Lost Opportunity,* from Christian Heritage Fellowship, https://christianheritagefellowship.com/d-l-moodys-lost-opportunity/Accessed 5/30/2016).

2   Adapted from Scott Bowles, "Hesitation Is a Fatal Mistake as California Firestorm Closes In," *USA Today,* October 30, 2003.

3   Charles Spurgeon, from a sermon dated 1887.

4   Bernard DeVoto, ed., *The Journals of Lewis and Clark* (Boston and New York: Houghton Mifflin Company, 1997 [1953]), p. 60.

ABOUT THE AUTHOR

CHARLES R. SWINDOLL has devoted his life to the accurate, practical teaching and application of God's Word and His grace. A pastor at heart, Chuck has served as senior pastor to congregations in Massachusetts, California, and Texas. Since 1998, he has served as the founder and senior pastor-teacher of Stonebriar Community Church in Frisco, Texas, but Chuck's listening audience extends far beyond a local church body. As a leading program in Christian broadcasting since 1979, *Insight for Living* airs in major Christian radio markets around the world, reaching people groups in languages they can understand. Chuck's extensive writing ministry has also served the body of Christ worldwide, and his leadership as president and now chancellor of Dallas Theological Seminary has helped prepare and equip a new generation of men and women for ministry. Chuck and Cynthia, his partner in life and ministry, have four grown children, ten grandchildren, and six great-grandchildren.

IF YOU ENJOYED THIS BOOK, WILL YOU CONSIDER SHARING THE MESSAGE WITH OTHERS?

Mention the book in a blog post or through Facebook, Twitter, Pinterest, or upload a picture through Instagram.

Recommend this book to those in your small group, book club, workplace, and classes.

Head over to facebook.com/worthypublishing, "LIKE" the page, and post a comment as to what you enjoyed the most.

Tweet "I recommend reading #FindingGodWhenTheWorldIsOnFire by @charlesswindoll // @worthypub"

Pick up a copy for someone you know who would be challenged and encouraged by this message.

Write a book review online.

WORTHY®
PUBLISHING

Visit us at worthypublishing.com

twitter.com/worthypub

worthypub.tumblr.com

facebook.com/worthypublishing

pinterest.com/worthypub

instagram.com/worthypub

youtube.com/worthypublishing